ONCE UPON A TIME

CONTENTS

FAREWELL, MOTHER! I'M OFF TO FACE DIRE PERILS IN THE WILDERNESS.

HAVE FUN, DEAR.

COUNTRY COTTAGE

Goodbye, home-sweet-home! Jack lives with his mother in a country cottage deep in the woods. Jack doesn't know what lies beyond the woods—but he can't wait to find out! (See p.6.)

TELLING A FAIRY TALE
BARNEY MAIN

"I really enjoyed working on my chapter, as I got to read loads of children's books as my research! I also used cartoons and history books for inspiration. I had a good idea of how I wanted each fairy tale model to look, but I made lots of changes as I went along. I especially like how the larger fairy tale characters (pp.10–11) came out, as I'd never built anything like them before."

WE CENTAURS HAVE NO NEED OF GOLD.

JACK'S JOURNEY

Little Jack has spent all his young life in one place and longs to have an adventure. When a cry goes up across the land that the King's Royal Nugget has been stolen, Jack knows that at last this is his chance to see the big, wide world. The King requests that all heroes in the kingdom go in search of the Royal Nugget. The one to return it to him will be granted a rich reward. Jack decides to pack his backpack and set out to find the Royal Nugget—and his fortune!

ALAS! WHERE COULD IT BE?

WOODLAND WONDERS

Jack discovers mythical woodland realms on his travels. Will the strange plants and creatures he finds there be his friends or his foes? (See p.8.)

NO NUGGET HERE, KID. SCRAM!

FEE-FI-FO-FUM, I'VE GOT SOME ROAST CHICKEN. YUM!

GIANT TROUBLE

Nowhere is out of reach for little Jack—even the kingdom of the giants, way up in the clouds. Will Jack become the giant's next dinner? (See p.16.)

TROLL TERROR

Jack's quest to find the Royal Nugget takes him over a troll-guarded bridge. Better run, Jack—that troll doesn't look too happy! (See p.14.)

SQUEAK!

FAIRY TALE COTTAGE

Jack is setting out on his adventure, and where better to start his story than the quaint country cottage where he grew up? A cottage is a nice place to stop and rest after a long day of walking. Will your cottage be on farmland, or deep in the woods? You could even make extra cottages and change their colors around to create an entire village!

This door was built first, then the frame was constructed around it

FRONT VIEW

Fancy window is the bottom of a small turntable piece

Latticed windows lend a rustic feel

A roof of stepped yellow bricks looks like it's made out of straw. Make sure it's built to support its own weight so it doesn't collapse!

Try building a secret hiding place inside your cottage's roof.

KITCHEN

Give your minifigures everything they could need, including the kitchen sink! In the cottage kitchen there are jars of food on the shelves, a powerful oven, and a nice mug of LEGO® broth waiting on the table.

The oven door is made from a tile with clips

Pose and accessorize your characters so they're doing something, like gardening or repairing the house

IT'S SO HARD TO KEEP A COTTAGE WARM WHEN IT SPLITS OPEN IN THE MIDDLE!

Flowers are a sign of a well-cared-for home

Use small tiles to make a tiled floor, or long brown ones for wooden floorboards

Cone bricks can be used for the legs of a chair, table, or stool

Tabletop is the base from a LEGO® Minifigures collectible character

COZY HOME

Building from reference can really inspire your choice of colors and shapes for your fairy tale cottage, so take a look at your favorite fairy tale books for ideas! Brown timber frames around white plaster walls give this building a half-timbered style.

LIVING SPACE

Fill your cottage with furniture and decorations that fit a pastoral setting, like a rug, a picture, and a fireplace. Use transparent orange elements to make a roaring fire, and have some firewood at the ready for when it starts to go out!

Attach a 1x4 tile to a 1x1 brick with side stud for a diagonal brown beam

What will your occupants need in their home? Build in details to suit your minifigures.

Stack white plates like a staircase to make a plume of puffy smoke

Use more than one hinge plate for strength and stability

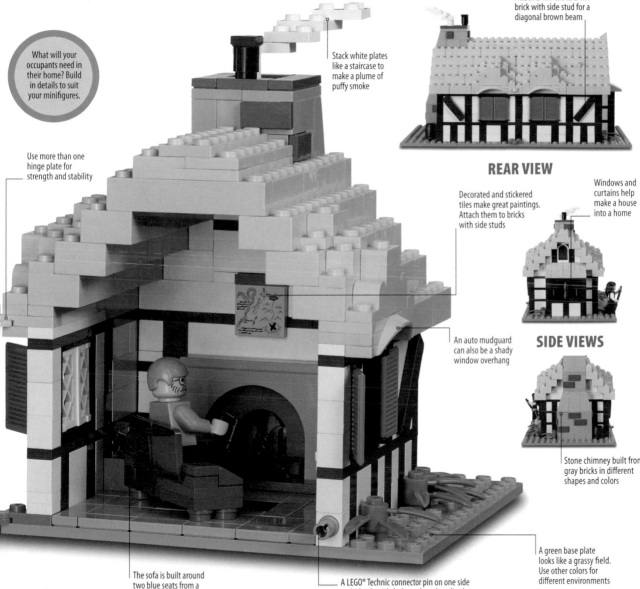

REAR VIEW

Decorated and stickered tiles make great paintings. Attach them to bricks with side studs

Windows and curtains help make a house into a home

An auto mudguard can also be a shady window overhang

SIDE VIEWS

Stone chimney built from gray bricks in different shapes and colors

The sofa is built around two blue seats from a LEGO vehicle model

A LEGO® Technic connector pin on one side and a brick-with-hole on the other clip the cottage together securely when it's closed

A green base plate looks like a grassy field. Use other colors for different environments

Arch elements are great for building spreading branches

Pull the chain to activate the hug of doom!

REAR VIEW

ENCHANTED FOREST

A walk in the woods sounded like fun, but Jack has gotten lost. Yikes, did that tree just move? Storybook forests are always full of mystery and adventure. They can be home to ferocious monsters and beasts, or helpful fairies and magical creatures. Build a forest with caves, rocks, rivers, and lots of trees in different shapes and sizes!

BUILDER TALK

"Getting the monster tree's arms to grab a minifigure was tricky. I came up with a technique that I'd never used before: the arms swing together when you pull on a chain that connects them."

What is this tree protecting? Or does it just not like minifigures?

If you don't have LEGO leaf pieces, use any green bricks and plates—or just leave the branches bare!

Pieces with unusual curves and shapes make a forest creation look organic and growing

Two barrels attached with LEGO Technic cross-axles make a pair of creepy, hollow eyes

HUG OF DOOM

The tree's grabbing arms are half-arch pieces built on their sides, with L-shaped plates for the branch-hands on the ends. They move on pivot points made with LEGO Technic bricks and axles.

Use slopes and bricks to build up the shape of a big, sturdy tree trunk

MONSTER TREE

This tree's arm-like branches can close to capture a LEGO minifigure. To make your own living tree, just build a regular one and then add creature features like eyes, hands, or even big pointy teeth!

Build in roots for a natural look

It doesn't matter what color pieces you use on the inside—they'll be hidden from view!

INSIDE THE PINE

This pine tree is built around a central core of bricks with studs on their sides, and plates attached to them sideways. Stacking more plates on the bottom creates a tapered shape.

Studs pointing outwards make the tree look bristly

PINE TREE

Some LEGO sets include single-piece pine trees, but you can build your own versions to plant in your forest! This pine tree is built to fit into the same base as the chopping tree below, so the two are interchangeable.

Try blue trees for a magical forest, or white for a snowy one.

Build realistic rocks out of gray slopes and tiles arranged in an uneven shape

SECRET SURPRISES

What would a fairy tale forest be without a few surprises? This "ratapult" launches a rat out of a hollow rock to scare unwary adventurers! You can build all kinds of fun tricks and traps into your forest creations.

CHOPPING TREE

Some people work in forests—even enchanted ones! A woodcutter makes his living by cutting down trees. This chopping tree is perfect for lumber as it's straight, tall, and thin enough to be cut up and hauled away. Its trunk is made from stacked 2x2 round bricks, with plant leaves built in.

Light green leaves look healthy and vibrant

OH BOY! I HOPE I GET MADE INTO SOMETHING REALLY COOL...LIKE A BATTERING RAM!

Build the trees for your forest with different heights and leaf patterns to make them look unique

A LEGO Technic towball inside the hollow base pushes up on the trunk to dislodge it

Push down here to topple the tree

TIMBER!

TOPPLING TREE

This tree is built with a special action feature: when you push down on the LEGO Technic towball at its base, it topples over as if the woodcutter has just chopped it down.

Stacked 2x2 round bricks

FOREST FLORA

Strolling through the woods, Jack spots all sorts of strange and wondrous things. Maybe getting lost isn't so bad after all! When building flowers and mushrooms for an enchanted forest, look at real plants for inspiration—but don't stop there. Let your imagination take root and grow by giving your creations new shapes, wild colors, and magical features.

Palm tree elements could also be the leaves of a big flower—or use green plates instead

For a low-lying flower, prop it up with a hinge plate instead of a long stem

REAR VIEW

Legend says this flower is allergic to frogs. Will one help your hero escape?

Sticking out of the center is a classic LEGO plant piece

BUILDING ROUND

A plate with an octagonal bar around it forms the center of this flower, with one petal clipped to each bar segment to create a circular flower shape. The three leaves clip onto 1x2 plates with bars that are attached underneath.

GIANT FLOWER

This big flower may have a lovely aroma, but don't get too close or it might fold its petals shut to catch you tight! The most important step in building a giant flower is finding the right piece to go in the middle. Look for parts that can connect to a ring of petals.

IT SMELLS SO NICE HERE. MAYBE I COULD TAKE A QUICK NAP...

Clip-and-bar connections let petals close in to catch a minifigure—or to form a fairy's bed!

Each petal is made from two pieces: an angled plate and a 1x1 plate with a clip on top

PETAL POWER

To build this flower, you only need a few types of LEGO pieces: a dinner plate element for the circular center, and a set of petals made from tooth plates attached to 1x1 plates with clips.

TALL FLOWERS

Flowers can be even more realistic if you build them on top of stems. It may be tricky to make a stem that is tall and thin, but also sturdy and well-balanced. Here are some different ways to create them.

Stacked 1x1 round bricks, with slope bricks for leaves

Petals are double angled plates connected to plates with clips, which clip on to handled bars around the center

Angled-plate leaves attach to a brick with side studs

FOREST FUNGI

Decorate your fairy tale forest with mushrooms and toadstools in many sizes and colors. You could make tiny ones with small radar dishes and round bricks, or build your own giant mushrooms like this one out of bigger bricks and plates.

Build from the top down, creating descending steps in all directions

Jumper plates help to line up the pieces at the bottom

Use textured bricks for a stalk

SPINNING FLOWER TOPS

In a magic forest, flowers don't have to be attached to the ground! Why not build a flower that can spin around like a spinning top? Build some with your friends and see whose spinning tops can spin the longest, travel the furthest, or knock the other forest flowers down.

Keep your flower's pieces balanced. A lopsided top doesn't spin as well as one with the same weight on all sides

Add vines and spikes to make a scary-looking battle flower top!

Flower leaves are green plate pieces

SIDE VIEW

SECURE SPIN

Push a LEGO Technic cross-axle through the center of your spinning top for a point on the bottom and a spinning-handle on top. Use bricks with axle holes through them to hold the cross-axle in place.

2x2 round brick has a hole for the cross-axle to pass through

Experiment with different colors and patterns of bricks

What will your colors look like when your top is spinning around?

SIDE VIEW

FAIRY TALE CREATURES

The world is an incredible place when you're on an adventure. Jack bumps into all kinds of amazing creatures on his quest! Animals and fantasy creatures bring lots of new storytelling possibilities to fairy tale models. You can add extra parts to your minifigures to make some, or build them entirely out of your bricks.

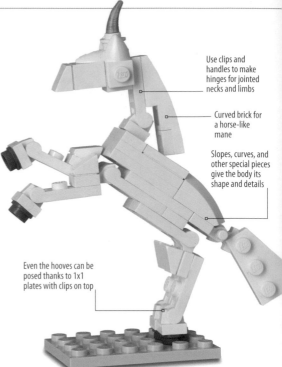

Use clips and handles to make hinges for jointed necks and limbs

Curved brick for a horse-like mane

Slopes, curves, and other special pieces give the body its shape and details

Even the hooves can be posed thanks to 1x1 plates with clips on top

UNICORNS

Unicorns are usually portrayed as white horses with horns growing from their foreheads. Beyond that, the details are up to you. This posable unicorn looks like it's ready for battle!

HONK!

FEATHERED FORM

The adult swan's wings are built separately to the body. They are made up of curved bricks on top, slope bricks below, and a stacked pair of tooth plates for feathers in the back.

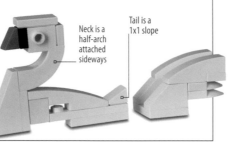

Neck is a half-arch attached sideways

Tail is a 1x1 slope

ELVES

Your stories can involve different kinds of elves, from tiny cobblers to tall and graceful warriors. These Fair Folk of the woods wear green and brown so they blend in with the trees. Will they help your hero or play mischievous tricks?

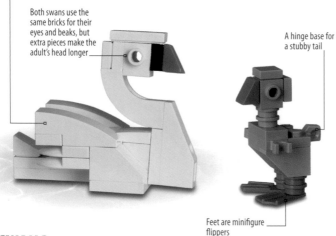

Both swans use the same bricks for their eyes and beaks, but extra pieces make the adult's head longer

A hinge base for a stubby tail

Feet are minifigure flippers

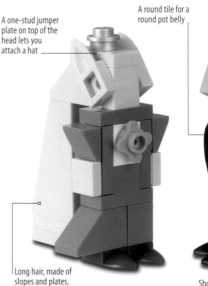

A one-stud jumper plate on top of the head lets you attach a hat

A round tile for a round pot belly

Long hair, made of slopes and plates, reaches the ground to support itself

Shoes are made from tooth plates

SWANS

Remember the ugly duckling that turned out to be a swan? You can build both! Baby animals often look cute and clumsy, with big heads, eyes, and feet. A grown-up swan should have graceful curves and smooth features.

ADVENTURE ACCESSORIES

Use your bricks to create unique items for your story's minifigures. For a staff, all you need is a long handle, antenna, or bar. Attach other elements to the end or clip them to the sides to make different styles.

WANT TO TRADE?

WELL, I DO HAPPEN TO HAVE THIS MYSTIC, TREASURE-FINDING STAFF...

A skull and ax blades make this look like a villain's weapon

You can include magical special effects, too!

A wise wizard might carry this ancient stone walking stick

This could be a sorcerer's staff...or add a flame in the middle for a tall torch

Try to match the colors of the hair piece and the horse body

DON'T BELIEVE HIM. THAT STAFF ONLY FINDS TURNIPS!

Is your centaur a scholar or a fighter? It's all in the choice of minifigure parts and accessories!

CENTAURS

Half-horse and half-human, these galloping creatures of myth can be created by building new four-legged lower bodies with two-stud attachments on top for minifigure torsos.

Two pairs of minifigure legs make great horse legs!

Round plates for hooves

Stacks of plates and bricks for legs—or make them posable like the unicorn's

QUESTS

As your heroes travel on their fairy tale adventure, they're sure to discover challenges that test their courage and skills. They might have to cross a rickety bridge high above a lava-filled chasm, face a monster in its den, or track down a king's missing treasure. Whatever quests you can imagine, you can make them come to life with your LEGO bricks.

MAGIC WELL

This could be an enchanted well that grants your wish if you drop in a brick. Or maybe it has a curse on it that turns anybody who drinks from it into a frog. Better ask the witch, to be on the safe side!

Roof shingles built from brown plates

Plates with clips make nice decorations

DOUBLE, DOUBLE, TOIL, AND TROUBLE... I'VE FORGOTTEN WHAT I PUT IN THIS ONE!

OKAY, I'VE GONE UP THE HILL AND FETCHED A PAIL OF WATER. NOW WHAT?

Make a deeper well by building your structure on a raised platform

For a bucket, you could also use a barrel or a 2x2 brick

Tiles on top hold the walls together

Bricks with side studs hold the roof at an angle on both sides

1x1 brick-with-hole

The round shape of the well is built with curved bricks

If you don't have a chain, try using a string

THE MAGIC REVEALED

Just turn the lance to wind up the chain and discover the magic potion inside the well. The lance goes through bricks with holes at the tops of the support posts, and has a cone over its end at the far side so it won't slide out.

Tan side-by-side 1x4 plates blend in with the rest of the surface

Strange plants and dangerous animals make a scene appear weird and foreboding

Skull and crossbones tile from a LEGO pirate game

I WONDER WHAT THAT SIGN SAYS. OH WELL, IT CAN'T BE TOO IMPORTANT.

Use brown pieces to make a dirt trap, or white for a pit full of snow.

QUICKSAND

In a fairy tale world, you never know where you'll encounter a trick or a trap. What looks like a stretch of solid ground might really be a treacherous pit full of quicksand!

It's a good thing this adventurer checked the sand with his walking stick first!

Pull this slider to release the trap

To reset the trap, just take the 1x4 plates out and push the slider back in again

ACTION VIEW

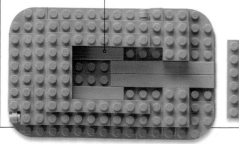

Smooth tiles keep trap pieces from snagging on studs when you slide it out

A T-shaped end keeps the slider from being pulled out too far

SAND, QUICK!

When you pull the plate with handle on the slider, the loose 1x4 plates that are resting on top fall into the deep pit beneath—taking anyone standing there along with them!

ARGHH!

TROLL BRIDGE

"Hold it right there! If you want to cross this bridge, you'll have to pay the troll." Jack has come upon a classic fairy tale peril: an evil troll that lives under a bridge. To get past it, he might have to solve a riddle, battle his way across, or distract the troll with a tasty snack. But step carefully, because this bridge has a built-in surprise!

Top plate rests on a thin lip at one end and smooth tiles at the other. Nudge it out of place and gravity takes care of the rest!

You could also make a hinged trap door or one that works like the quicksand trap on p.13.

TRAP DOOR

Step in the wrong spot on top of the bridge and the secret hatch falls down, sending you tumbling into the clutches of the troll below! Some LEGO sets include trap door elements, but you can also build your own in whatever style you like.

THE BRIDGE

A bridge should be built like an arch—good and strong. This one is made out of dark gray bricks with lighter gray bricks for accent stonework. Tan bricks form steps to let a minifigure (or goat) walk up and across the span.

I CAN SEE MY HOUSE FROM HERE!

A 2x4 double angled plate for a keystone

1x1 slopes turn jagged bumps into smooth curves

Use an antenna or spear with a round brick on the end to make bulrushes

Include wetlands details such as muddy banks, plants, and frogs

Does your bridge go over water? Then build a base of transparent and solid blue plates!

TROLL

This mean-tempered troll is big enough to bully a minifigure, but small enough to hide under the bridge. Add a plate with clip to his hand so he can hold a spiked club— and shake it angrily at any trespassers!

WHO'S WALKING ON MY BRIDGE? I'LL GOBBLE THEM UP, BRICKS AND ALL!

TROLLISH FEATURES

Four headlight bricks with hollow side studs make up most of the troll's square head. His little round nose is a folded-up hinge plate.

Horn pieces from a LEGO cow plug into the headlight bricks' hollow studs

Eyes are round plates from a LEGO® Games set

Hinge plate

Spiked club comes from the LEGO Minifigures line

Arms are built out of hinges, clips, and plates with handles

Clawed fingers and toes are made from tooth plates

Legs are made from 2x2 round bricks and plates

Set one foot in front of the other for a sense of movement and action

Big feet make a two-legged model more stable

FRONT SIDE VIEW

QUICK BUILD

BILLY GOATS GRUFF

Each of these three billy goat brothers is bigger and tougher than the last. You can build them in two shakes of a goat's tail if you have similar pieces! First design your goat's head, then use slopes or arches lined with plates for the body, and cones and round plates for legs and feet.

Tail piece used as a horn

Include features in common, like headlight brick eyes and little clippity-clop hooves

You can use these same techniques to make little versions of big animals or big versions of little ones!

Attach cow horns to 1x1 round plates with open studs

Don't forget a beard for the biggest billy goat

Horn piece for a stubby tail

Hooves are flowers with open studs

GIANTS

When Jack climbed up a beanstalk, he never expected that he'd discover a land in the clouds, much less one filled with hungry giants! If you're tired of tussling with trolls, then try a giant on for size. These fee-fi-fo-fearsome creatures are really tough because they can be as smart as a human (or a minifigure), but they're a whole lot bigger and stronger.

BIG HEAD

There are lots of ways to build your giant's head. Experiment with your pieces to find the features and expression you like the most. This giant's grinning face uses bracket pieces for the sides of the mouth, and round tiles for the nose and cheeks.

Mass of black slopes and tooth plates for messy hair

Use red or black bricks for the inside of the mouth

White slopes for teeth—leave one out for a gap-toothed grin!

A row of forward-facing clips makes a shaggy mono-brow

Eyes are hollow-stud 1x1 round plates from LEGO Games sets

EVIL GIANT

Better run, Jack—this giant's legs are a lot longer than yours! They are attached to LEGO Technic bricks with ball joints to make them posable. All giants are tall, but they are also individuals, so give your giants all kinds of different faces, clothes, and body shapes.

Bones for shirt toggles

Use ball-and-socket pieces from LEGO buildable action figures to create articulated arms

A giant-sized belt to hold up giant-sized pants!

Tunic is shaped by slope bricks

SIDE VIEW

JUST THE RIGHT SIZE FOR A LIGHT SNACK!

EEK!

You can also use basic bricks and hinges for bendable arms

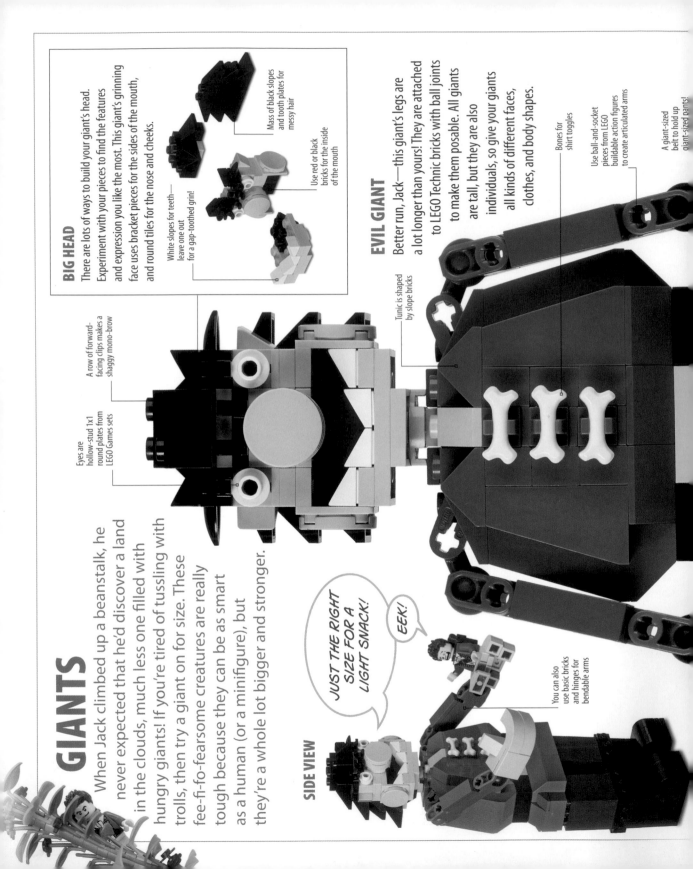

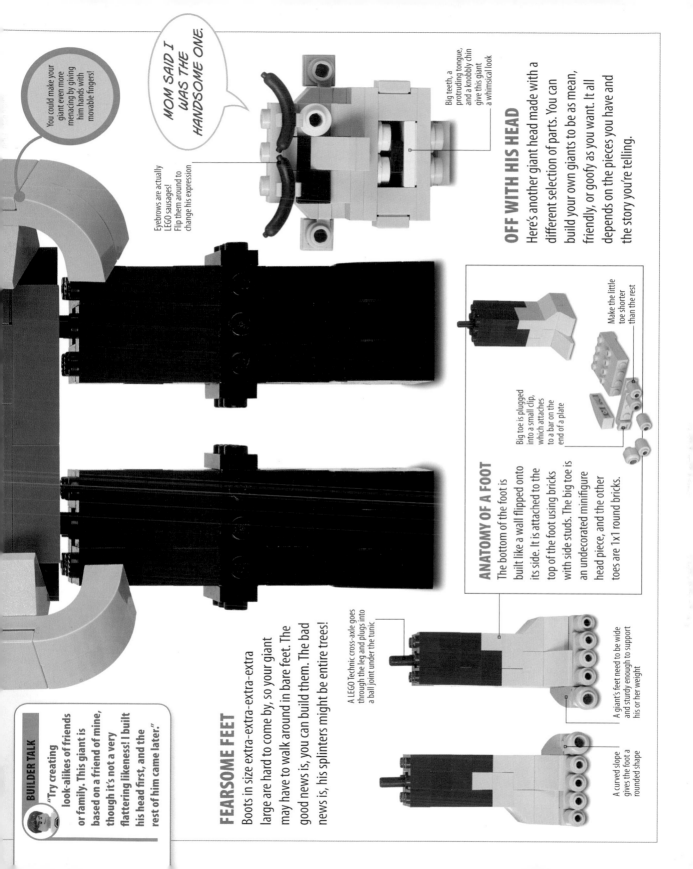

You could make your giant even more menacing by giving him hands with movable fingers!

MOM SAID I WAS THE HANDSOME ONE.

Eyebrows are actually LEGO sausages! Flip them around to change his expression

Big teeth, a protruding tongue, and a knobbly chin give this giant a whimsical look

OFF WITH HIS HEAD

Here's another giant head made with a different selection of parts. You can build your own giants to be as mean, friendly, or goofy as you want. It all depends on the pieces you have and the story you're telling.

Make the little toe shorter than the rest

Big toe is plugged into a small clip, which attaches to a bar on the end of a plate

ANATOMY OF A FOOT

The bottom of the foot is built like a wall flipped onto its side. It is attached to the top of the foot using bricks with side studs. The big toe is an undecorated minifigure head piece, and the other toes are 1x1 round bricks.

A LEGO Technic cross-axle goes through the leg and plugs into a ball joint under the tunic

A giant's feet need to be wide and sturdy enough to support his or her weight

A curved slope gives the foot a rounded shape

"Try creating look-alikes of friends or family. This giant is based on a friend of mine, though it's not a very flattering likeness! I built his head first, and the rest of him came later."

FEARSOME FEET

Boots in size extra-extra-extra-extra large are hard to come by, so your giant may have to walk around in bare feet. The good news is, you can build them. The bad news is, his splinters might be entire trees!

GIANT'S KITCHEN

As Jack explores the land of the giants, he starts to feel a bit like a mouse. Everything here is so huge! Don't just build a giant for your adventure—construct a whole world for it. What kind of furniture and tools would exist in a giant's home? Does your giant use regular-sized objects in new ways, like a sword for a butter knife or a lion for a house pet?

ROAST CHICKEN

For an appetizing dinner, use curved bricks and tiles to hide the studs. LEGO Technic pins let the drumsticks attach at an angle, and pop right off if your giant is feeling hungry!

LEGO dinner plates will work for small dishes, but for big ones, make your own!

NOW WHERE HAS THAT LITTLE MORSEL GONE?

CHAIR

Can you match the look of your table and chairs? This chair has a wooden frame of brown bricks and plates, with tan grilles in the seat to make a wicker pattern. Just like the table, the legs are topped with minifigure skulls.

A radar dish, an antenna, and a dome make a fine candlestick

A green LEGO® EXO-FORCE™ hair piece resembles a leafy head of cabbage

Bones are the remains of previous meals

A whole barrel can be a giant's drinking cup

GULP

Tabletop made from overlapping plates

DINNER TABLE

Building a giant table is just like building a small one: it needs four sturdy legs and a big flat top. Look for the biggest pieces in your collection, or assemble it in sections from lots of small bricks.

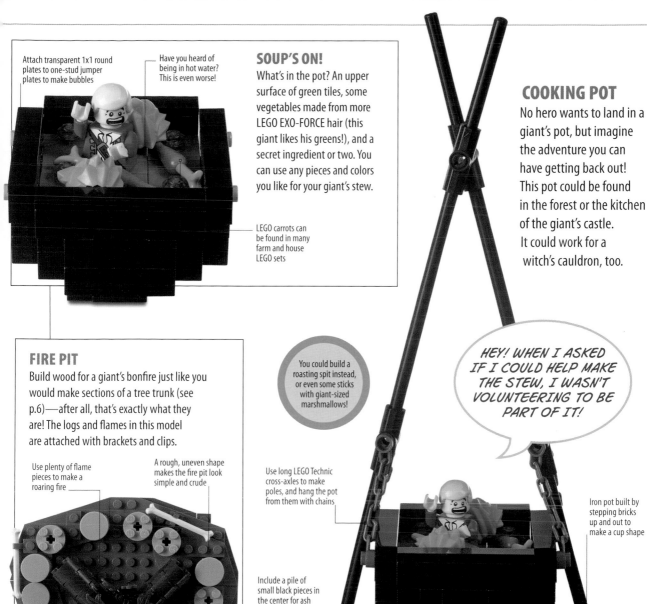

Attach transparent 1x1 round plates to one-stud jumper plates to make bubbles

Have you heard of being in hot water? This is even worse!

SOUP'S ON!

What's in the pot? An upper surface of green tiles, some vegetables made from more LEGO EXO-FORCE hair (this giant likes his greens!), and a secret ingredient or two. You can use any pieces and colors you like for your giant's stew.

LEGO carrots can be found in many farm and house LEGO sets

COOKING POT

No hero wants to land in a giant's pot, but imagine the adventure you can have getting back out! This pot could be found in the forest or the kitchen of the giant's castle. It could work for a witch's cauldron, too.

FIRE PIT

Build wood for a giant's bonfire just like you would make sections of a tree trunk (see p.6)—after all, that's exactly what they are! The logs and flames in this model are attached with brackets and clips.

You could build a roasting spit instead, or even some sticks with giant-sized marshmallows!

HEY! WHEN I ASKED IF I COULD HELP MAKE THE STEW, I WASN'T VOLUNTEERING TO BE PART OF IT!

Use plenty of flame pieces to make a roaring fire

A rough, uneven shape makes the fire pit look simple and crude

Use long LEGO Technic cross-axles to make poles, and hang the pot from them with chains

Iron pot built by stepping bricks up and out to make a cup shape

Include a pile of small black pieces in the center for ash and charcoal

Build up the outside of the pit with angled plates and round bricks to contain the blaze

1x1 round plates for eyes

Angle plate hair

Stacked 2x2 round plates make a simple face

PLAY OPTIONS

Think about how you want to play with your brick character. Build some extra body parts to swap in and give your characters different looks and poses. This knight also has an unhelmeted head for when he doesn't have to stand guard at the castle!

There are lots of ways to build a helmet. Create some different designs of your own!

Armour built out of curved and angled pieces

FAIRY TALE CHARACTERS

Your fairy tale doesn't have to just star minifigures. You can use your bricks to build bigger and more detailed characters, too. They can be as colourful and as fantastical as you like! You can even mix them in scenes with minifigures so they become super-sized heroes.

Side stud bricks for hands allow the knight to hold his sword and shield

Sword blade is a long, round column, but you could build a stack of 1x1 round bricks

Small radar dish for the shield's central boss

Cape attaches to the body at three points

KNIGHT

Start out a brick character with the basics – a head, two arms, two legs, and a body – and then add any other parts you want. This knight is equipped with a sword, a shield, a cape and a helmet with a fancy feather plume.

Calves are grey minifigure heads

REAR VIEW

A cape should be narrow at the top and wider at the bottom

Cape is too heavy to attach it solely at the shoulders, so build it into the body

BRICKS IN MOTION

Solid bricks can be used to create dynamic motion. The knight's cape is built just like a LEGO brick wall, with slopes and inverted slopes to give it a swooshing shape, as if it is being blown by the wind.

Neat and tidy hairdo made from arch pieces

Push the stud of a 1x1 round plate into a brick-with-hole for a fine button. Try designing your own royal fashions!

THE CROWN JEWELS

It's easy to make a crown fit for a queen. This one has 1x1 plates with clips attached to a 1x1 brick with studs on its sides. When building royalty, make sure your costumes look rich and fancy.

Add height to the crown with a cone piece

A plate with octagonal bar makes a wide collar ruff

QUEEN

This queen has a different body shape than the knight, but she is built in the same style and scale, so she looks like she comes from the same fairy tale. You could make your characters tall and thin, short and stout — or anything in between!

NICE TO MEET YOU, YOUR MAJESTY.

Posable arms are attached to headlight bricks on the body with tap pieces for shoulders

A row of 1x1 plates with clips pointing forwards and back gives the bottom of the queen's dress a lacy, frilly look

REAR VIEW

QUICK BUILD

A wizard needs a staff — this one is made from a bar and two cones

Pointy hat made from plates and a cone, topped off with a 1x1 round plate

1x2 plate with click hinge for a big nose

WIZARD

You don't need a magic wand to build this model! A simple wizard can be built in a flash if you have similar pieces. Slope bricks build up the majority of the body and the hair.

Create a cloak with a car roof

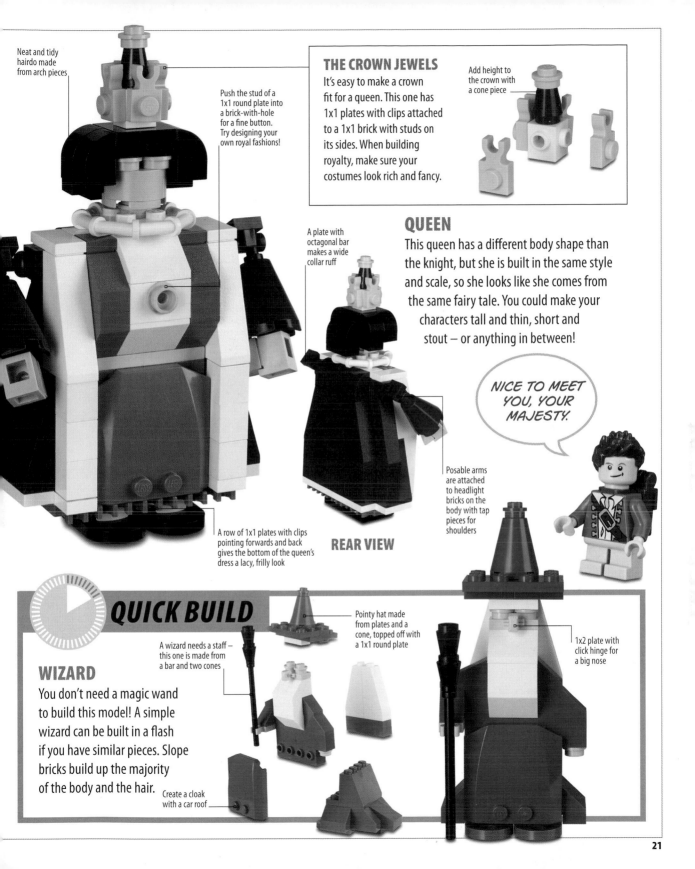

UNDERSEA CHARACTERS

While taking a swim, Jack is so surprised that he almost forgets to hold his breath…there are people living under the sea! The seas of a fairy tale world are brimming with mythical, magical creatures, from krakens and sea serpents to mermaids and mermen. If you don't have any mer-minifigures, don't flounder about—use your bricks to build some!

MY HAIRSTYLE? I LIKE TO GO FOR THE WET LOOK.

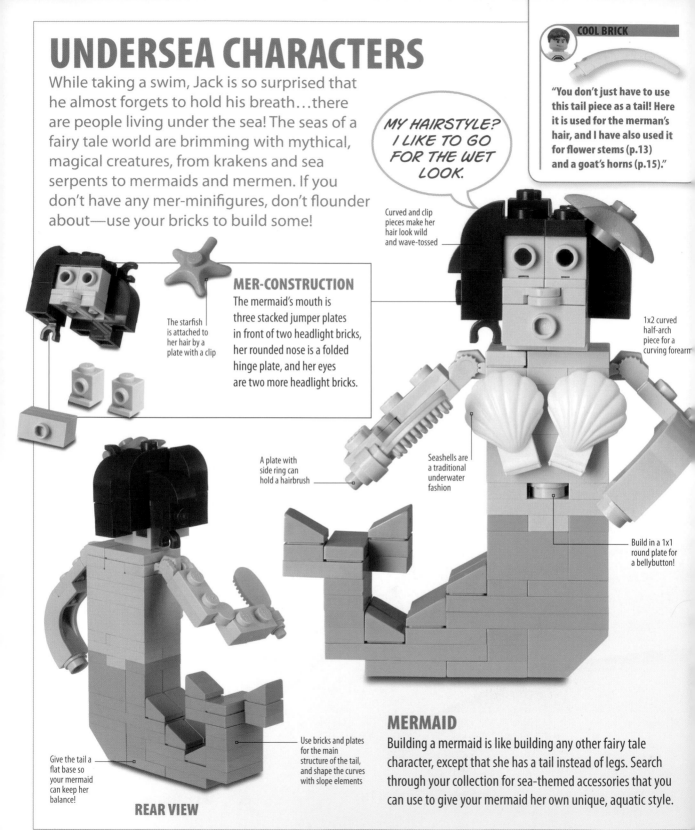

Curved and clip pieces make her hair look wild and wave-tossed

1x2 curved half-arch piece for a curving forearm

The starfish is attached to her hair by a plate with a clip

MER-CONSTRUCTION

The mermaid's mouth is three stacked jumper plates in front of two headlight bricks, her rounded nose is a folded hinge plate, and her eyes are two more headlight bricks.

A plate with side ring can hold a hairbrush

Seashells are a traditional underwater fashion

Build in a 1x1 round plate for a bellybutton!

Use bricks and plates for the main structure of the tail, and shape the curves with slope elements

Give the tail a flat base so your mermaid can keep her balance!

REAR VIEW

MERMAID

Building a mermaid is like building any other fairy tale character, except that she has a tail instead of legs. Search through your collection for sea-themed accessories that you can use to give your mermaid her own unique, aquatic style.

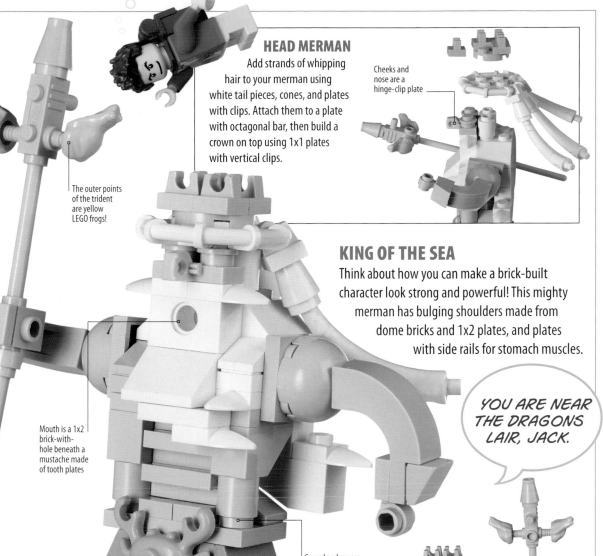

HEAD MERMAN

Add strands of whipping hair to your merman using white tail pieces, cones, and plates with clips. Attach them to a plate with octagonal bar, then build a crown on top using 1x1 plates with vertical clips.

Cheeks and nose are a hinge-clip plate

The outer points of the trident are yellow LEGO frogs!

KING OF THE SEA

Think about how you can make a brick-built character look strong and powerful! This mighty merman has bulging shoulders made from dome bricks and 1x2 plates, and plates with side rails for stomach muscles.

Mouth is a 1x2 brick-with-hole beneath a mustache made of tooth plates

YOU ARE NEAR THE DRAGONS LAIR, JACK.

Curved and square pieces provide muscle definition

This tail is built more simply than the mermaid's, using 1x2 slopes to make the curved shape at the end

An armored crab makes an intimidating ornament

REAR VIEW

DRAGON

Jack never dreamed that his search for the Royal Nugget would lead him to the cave of a fire-breathing dragon! He will have to rely on all of his luck and courage (and some help from a fearless dragon catcher) to get out of this in one piece. Defeating a dragon can be the ultimate quest for a hero. Build yours with lots of teeth, scales, and spikes—and don't forget a big pair of wings.

Gems aren't just for treasure—these ones make the dragon's big, glowing eyes!

Horn elements can attach to clips and bricks with hollow studs to make spikes and frills

FIRE BREATH

Smaller LEGO flame pieces plug into small brick holes, and bigger ones can attach to LEGO Technic cross-axle holes. Build pieces with attachment points into your dragon's head for a fiery-breath attack!

Neck joints are made with clips and handles

HEY, BIG AND SCALY! LOOK OVER HERE!

BUILDING A DRAGON

You can build a dragon in any size, shape, or color—it's your fairy tale! Design your dragon's head first, and then the neck and body. Add a tail, wings, and legs next, making sure it isn't too heavy or off-balance to stand up. Then give it lots of spikes and other ferocious details!

What reason will your hero have to brave the dragon's lair?

Add taloned toes to your dragon's feet

Surely the dragon won't be able to resist this dragon catcher's delicious bait?

Look through your collection for gold and silver elements, jewels, swords, crowns, and other precious items

HEAD DESIGNS

The dragon's head can inspire the rest of the body, so it's a good place to start building. Here are some head ideas for a long-horned blue dragon, an Asian-style green dragon, and a majestic golden dragon.

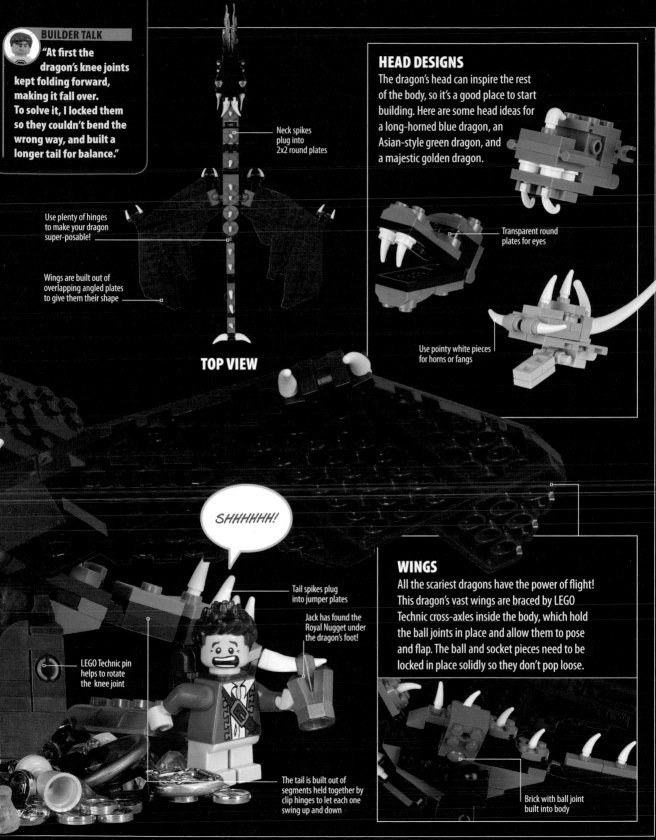

Neck spikes plug into 2x2 round plates

Use plenty of hinges to make your dragon super-posable!

Wings are built out of overlapping angled plates to give them their shape

TOP VIEW

Transparent round plates for eyes

Use pointy white pieces for horns or fangs

SHHHHHH!

Tail spikes plug into jumper plates

Jack has found the Royal Nugget under the dragon's foot!

LEGO Technic pin helps to rotate the knee joint

The tail is built out of segments held together by clip hinges to let each one swing up and down

WINGS

All the scariest dragons have the power of flight! This dragon's vast wings are braced by LEGO Technic cross-axles inside the body, which hold the ball joints in place and allow them to pose and flap. The ball and socket pieces need to be locked in place solidly so they don't pop loose.

Brick with ball joint built into body

FAIRY TALE CASTLE

Recovering the Royal Nugget has earned Jack an invitation to the king's castle. While real medieval castles were usually built to keep enemy armies out, and were more practical than beautiful, the castle of a fairy tale kingdom can be colorful and ornate. Give it elegant peaked turrets, festive flags and banners, and decorative designs that show off the magic and majesty of your fantasy kingdom.

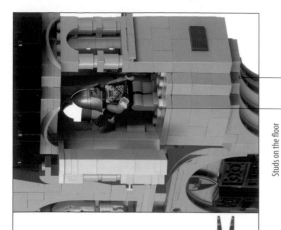

TURRET

Make your castle's turrets hollow with strong walls and an opening door so you can easily place minifigures inside. Will you put a palace guard or a captured prisoner in there?

Arches support the weight of the turrets from underneath

Studs on the floor stop the door from swinging too far in

Turret cones are built from the top down, stepping out each lower layer

Battlement crenellations are 1x2 bricks topped with 1x1 slopes

Pennant flags can be found in castle-themed LEGO sets—or build your own out of plates and clips!

Bricks in the middle of the turret cone keep it strong

Alternate round and square pieces to make columns around windows

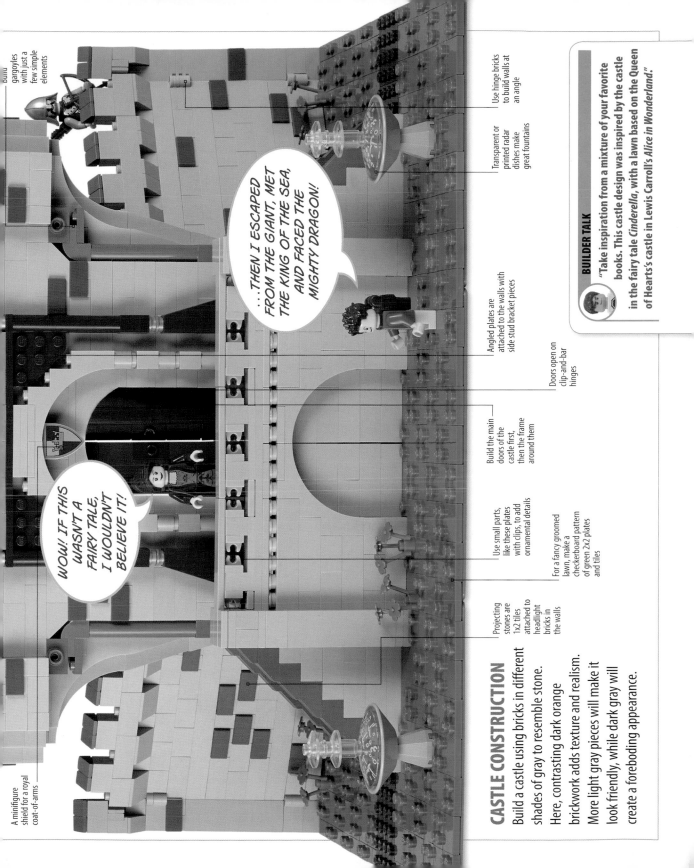

CASTLE CONSTRUCTION

Build a castle using bricks in different shades of gray to resemble stone. Here, contrasting dark orange brickwork adds texture and realism. More light gray pieces will make it look friendly, while dark gray will create a foreboding appearance.

A minifigure shield for a royal coat-of-arms

Build gargoyles with just a few simple elements

Use hinge bricks to build walls at an angle

Transparent or printed radar dishes make great fountains

Angled plates are attached to the walls with side stud bracket pieces

Doors open on clip-and-bar hinges

Build the main doors of the castle first, then the frame around them

Use small parts, like these plates with clips, to add ornamental details

For a fancy groomed lawn, make a checkerboard pattern of green 2x2 plates and tiles

Projecting stones are 1x2 tiles attached to headlight bricks in the walls

WOW! IF THIS WASN'T A FAIRY TALE, I WOULDN'T BELIEVE IT!

...THEN I ESCAPED FROM THE GIANT, MET THE KING OF THE SEA, AND FACED THE MIGHTY DRAGON!

BUILDER TALK

"Take inspiration from a mixture of your favorite books. This castle design was inspired by the castle in the fairy tale *Cinderella*, with a lawn based on the Queen of Hearts's castle in Lewis Carroll's *Alice in Wonderland*."

HANDFUL OF BRICKS LIST

4x4 plate x 1

2x2 inverted slope x 1

2x2 brick x 3

2 x 4 brick x 2

2x2 plate x 2

1x2/1x4 angle plate x1

1x6 plate x 2

2x2 slope x 3

Antenna x1

1x2 slope x 2

2x3 slope x 1

1x1 slope x 4

1x1 brick eyes x 2

1x2 tile with top bar x 1

1x2 plate x 1

1x2 plate x 1

2x4 angled plate x 2

1x1 round brick x 1

1x3 brick x 2

1x2 curved
half-arch x 1

4x4 round plate x 1

2x2 round brick x 1

Penguin Random House

For DK Publishing
Project Editor Hannah Dolan
Senior Designer Guy Harvey
Editors Jo Casey, Matt Jones, Victoria Taylor
Designers Jill Bunyan, Sam Richiardi, Lauren Rosier, Rhys Thomas
Jacket Designer David McDonald
Senior DTP Designer Kavita Varma
Pre-production Producer Siu Chan
Producer Lloyd Robertson
Managing Editor Simon Hugo
Design Manager Guy Harvey
Creative Manager Sarah Harland
Art Director Lisa Lanzarini
Publisher Julie Ferris
Publishing Director Simon Beecroft

For the LEGO Group
Project Manager Mikkel Joachim Petersen
Assistant Licensing Manager Randi Kirsten Sørensen
Senior Licensing Manager Corinna van Delden
Designer Melody Louise Caddick
Building Instruction Developer Alexandra Martin
Model makers Stephen Berry, Yvonne Doyle, Rod Gillies,
Tim Goddard, Tim Johnson, Barney Main, Pete Reid

Photography by Gary Ombler
First published in the United States in 2015 by DK Publishing
345 Hudson Street, New York, New York 10014

Contains material previously published in LEGO® *Play Book* (2013)

001—284611—Mar/15

Page design copyright © 2015 Dorling Kindersley Limited.
A Penguin Random House Company.

A catalog record for this book is available from the Library of Congress.

ISBN: 978-5-0010-1306-8

Printed in China.

www.dk.com
www.LEGO.com

Acknowledgments
Dorling Kindersley would like to thank: Randi Sørensen, Mikkel Petersen,
Melody Caddick, Corinna van Delden, and Alexandra Martin at the LEGO Group;
Stephen Berry, Yvonne Doyle, Rod Gillies, Tim Goddard, Tim Johnson, Barney Main,
Pete Reid, and Andrew Walker for their amazing models; Daniel Lipkowitz for his inspiring
text; Gary Ombler for his endless patience and brilliant photography; and Emma Grange,
Lauren Nesworthy, Lisa Stock, and Matt Wilson for editorial and design assistance.

A WORLD OF IDEAS:
SEE ALL THERE IS TO KNOW

1x1 brick x 7

4x6 plate x 1

1x1 headlight brick x 2

1x4 brick x 6

1x2 brick x 5
(including 1 transparent)

1x6 brick x 2

2x3 brick x 1

1x2 jumper plate x 3

1x2x1 panel x1

1x1 round plate x 2

1x4 plate x 2

2x2 radar dish x 2

Wide rim, wide tire,
and 2x2 axle plate
with 1 pin x 4

1x1 cone x 1

2x6 plate x 3

1x1 plate x 4

1x2 grille plate x 2

2x4 plate x 2

Faucet x 1

1x6 arch brick x 1

2x2 round plate x 2

4x4 radar dish x 1